Inspiration Revisited

presents

AS YOU THINK

A Reworking of
AS A MAN THINKETH
BY
JAMES ALLEN

*Mind is the Master power that moulds and makes,
And Have a Mind, and evermore you take
The tool of Thought, and, shaping what you will,
Brings forth a thousand joys, a thousand ills:—
You think in secret, and it comes to pass:
Environment is but your looking-glass.*

Edited Version

Copyright © 2020 Inspiration Revisited

All rights reserved.

Cover Image by Gerd Altmann from Pixabay

For all lovers of Inspirational Writing

FOREWORD	1
THOUGHT AND CHARACTER	3
EFFECT OF THOUGHT ON CIRCUMSTANCES	7
EFFECT OF THOUGHT ON HEALTH AND THE BODY	21
THOUGHT AND PURPOSE	25
THE THOUGHT-FACTOR IN ACHIEVEMENT	29
VISIONS AND IDEALS	33
SERENITY	39

ACKNOWLEDGEMENTS

Without Inspirational Works from the past, we would have a less colourful view of life. James Allen's diminutive tome, I hope, can now inspire a new generation.

FOREWORD

James Allen's original forward stated that this diminutive volume is not intended as an exhaustive discourse on the much-written-upon subject of the power of thought. It is suggestive rather than explanatory, its object being to stimulate every reader to the discovery and perception of the truth that - **"They are makers of themselves."** by virtue of the thoughts that they choose and encourage; that mind is the master weaver, both of the inner garment of character and the outer garment of circumstance, and that, as they may have up till now woven in ignorance and pain they may now weave in enlightenment and happiness.

Inspiration Revisited has utilized this small volume to create an updated version for modern times hopefully without losing its delightful original flavour. It has also been degenderized as far as possible and transposed into 'third person' to increase the power it has to influence the reader in a positive way. It is also available in 'first person' format should you feel that is more effective. Some of us like to advise ourselves of what to do others prefer to be told, whichever you have a preference for the authors hope you gain personal inspiration, and more, from revisiting this remarkable masterpiece.

THOUGHT AND CHARACTER

THE adage, "As a man thinks in his heart so is he," or, "As you think in your heart so are you," not only embraces the whole of your being but is so comprehensive as to reach out to every condition and circumstance of your life. You are literally *what you think,* your character being the complete sum of all your thoughts.

As the plant springs from, and could not be without the seed, so your every act springs from the hidden seeds of thought, and could not have appeared without them. This applies equally to those acts called "spontaneous" and "unpremeditated" as to those, which are deliberately executed.

Act is the blossom of thought, and joy and suffering are its fruits; thus do you gather in the sweet and bitter fruitage of your own husbandry.

"Thought in the mind has made you, What you are
By thought was wrought and built. If your mind
Has evil thoughts, pain comes on you as comes
The wheel the ox behind...

...If one endure
In purity of thought, joy follows you
As your own shadow—sure."

You are grown by law, and not created by deceit, and cause and effect are as absolute and undeviating in the hidden realm of thought as in the world of visible and material things. A noble and exceptional character is not a thing of favour or chance, but is the natural result of continued effort in right thinking, the effect of long-cherished association with exceptional thoughts. An ignoble and bestial character, by the same process, is the result of the continued harbouring of debasing thoughts.

You are made or unmade by yourself; in the armoury of thought you forge the weapons by which you destroy yourself; you also fashion the tools with which you build for yourself heavenly mansions of joy and strength and peace. By the right choice and true application of thought, you ascend to the Divine Perfection; by the abuse and wrong application of thought, you would descend below the level of the beast. Between these two extremes are all the grades of character, and you are their maker and master.

Of all the beautiful truths pertaining to the soul which have been restored and brought to light in this age, none are more gladdening or fruitful of divine promise and confidence than this—that you are the master of thought, the moulder of character, and the maker and shaper of your condition, environment, and destiny.

As a being of Power, Intelligence, and Love, and

the lord of your own thoughts, you hold the key to every situation and contain within yourself that transforming and regenerative agency by which you may make yourself what you will.

You are always the master, even in your weakest and most abandoned state; but in your weakness and degradation you are the foolish master who misgoverns your "household." When you begin to reflect upon your condition, and to search diligently for the Law upon which your being is established, you then become the wise master, directing your energies with intelligence, and fashioning your thoughts to fruitful issues. Such is the *conscious* master, and you can only thus become by discovering *within yourself* the laws of thought; which discovery is totally a matter of application, self-analysis, and experience.

Only by much searching and mining, are gold and diamonds obtained, and you can find every truth connected with your being if you will dig deep into the mine of your soul; and be aware that you are the maker of your character, the moulder of your life, and the builder of your destiny, you may unerringly prove, if you will watch, control, and alter your thoughts, tracing the effects upon yourself, upon others, and upon your life and circumstances, linking cause and effect by patient practise and investigation, and utilizing your every experience, even to the most trivial, everyday occurrence, as a means of obtaining that knowledge of yourself which is Understanding, Wisdom and Power. In this direction, as in no other, is the law absolute that "seek and you will find; knock it shall be opened to you;" for only by patience, practise, and ceaseless insistence can you enter the Door of the Temple of Knowledge.

EFFECT OF THOUGHT ON CIRCUMSTANCES

YOUR mind could be likened to a garden, which may be intelligently cultivated or allowed to run wild; but whether cultivated or neglected, it must, and will, *bring forth*. If no useful seeds are *put* into it, then an abundance of useless weed seeds will *fall* therein and will continue to produce their kind.

Just as a gardener cultivates a plot, keeping it free from weeds, and growing the flowers and fruits which they require, so may a you tend the garden of your mind, weeding out all the wrong, useless, and impure thoughts, and cultivating toward perfection the flowers and fruits of right, useful, and pure thoughts. By pursuing this process, you will, sooner or later, discover that you are the master gardener of your soul, the director of your life. You also reveal, within yourself, the laws of thought, and understand, with ever-increasing accuracy, how the thought-forces and mind elements operate in the shaping of your character, circumstances, and destiny.

Thought and character are one, and as your character can only manifest and discover itself through environment and circumstance, the outer conditions of your life will always be found to be harmoniously related to your inner state. This does not mean that your circumstances at any given time are an indication of your *entire* character, but that those circumstances are so intimately connected with some vital thought-element within yourself that, for the time being, they are indispensable to your development.

You are where you are by the law of your being; the thoughts which you have built into your character have brought you there, and in the arrangement of your life there is no element of chance, but all is the result of a law which cannot err. This is just as true as when you feel "out of harmony" with your surroundings as when you are contented with them.

As a progressive and evolving being, you are where you are that you may learn that you may grow; and as you learn the lesson which any circumstance contains for you, it passes away and gives place to other circumstances.

You are buffeted by circumstances so long as you believe yourself to be the creature of outside conditions, but when you realize that you are a creative power and that you may command the hidden soil and seeds of your being out of which circumstances grow, you then become the rightful master of yourself.

That circumstances grow out of thought, you would realise this if for any length of time you practised self-control and self-purification, for you will have noticed that the alteration in your circumstances has been in exact ratio with your altered mental condition. So true is this that when you earnestly apply yourself to remedy the defects in your character and make swift and marked progress, you pass rapidly through a succession of transformations.

The soul attracts that which it secretly harbours; that which it loves, and also that which it fears; it reaches the height of its cherished aspirations; it falls to the level of its unchaste desires,—and circumstances are the means by which your soul receives its own.

Every thought-seed sown or allowed to fall into your mind, and to take root there, produces its own, blossoming sooner or later into the act, and bearing its own fruitage of opportunity and circumstance. Good thoughts bear good fruit, bad thoughts bad fruit.

The outer world of circumstance shapes itself to the inner world of thought, and both pleasant and unpleasant external conditions are factors, which make for your ultimate good. As the reaper of your own harvest, you learn both by suffering and bliss.

Following the inmost desires, aspirations, thoughts, by which you allow yourself to be dominated, (pursuing the will-o'-the-wisps of impure imaginings or steadfastly walking the highway of strong and high endeavour), you, at last, arrive at the fruition and fulfilment in the outer conditions of your life. The laws of growth and adjustment are everywhere revealed.

You do not come to poverty or jail by the tyranny of fate or circumstance but by the pathway of debased thoughts and base desires. Nor do you, as a pure-minded person, fall suddenly into crime by stress of any mere external force; the criminal thought must have long been secretly fostered in your heart, and the hour of opportunity revealed its gathered power. Circumstances do not make you; they reveal themselves to you. No such conditions can exist as descending into vice and its attendant sufferings apart from vicious inclinations, or ascending into virtue and its pure happiness without the continued cultivation of virtuous aspirations; and you, therefore, as the lord and master of your thoughts, are the creator of yourself, the shaper and author of your environment. Even at birth, your soul came to its own and through every step of its earthly pilgrimage it attracts the combinations of conditions which reveal itself, which are the reflections of your own purity and, impurity, your strength and weakness.

You do not attract that which you *want,* but that which you *are.* Your whims, fancies, and ambitions are thwarted at every step, but your innermost thoughts and desires are fed with your own food, be it foul or clean. The "divinity that shapes your ends" are in yourself; it is your very self. Only you shackle yourself: thought and action are the gaolers of Fate—they imprison, being base; they are also the angels of Freedom—they liberate, being noble. Not what you wish and pray for do you get, but what you justly earn. Your wishes and prayers are only gratified and answered when they harmonize with your thoughts and actions.

In the light of this truth, what, then, is the meaning of "fighting against circumstances?" It means that you are continually rebelling against an *effect* without, while all the time you are nourishing and preserving its *cause* in your heart. That cause may take the form of a conscious vice or an unconscious weakness; but whatever it is, it stubbornly retards your efforts, and thus calls aloud for remedy.

You are anxious to improve your circumstances, but am unwilling to improve yourself; you, therefore, remain bound. But, if you do not shrink from self-sacrifice you can never fail to accomplish the object upon which your heart is set. This is as true of earthly as of lofty things. Even if your sole purpose is to acquire wealth you must be prepared to make great personal sacrifices before you can accomplish your objective; and how much more so if you would realize a strong and well-poised life?

For example, here is a person who is wretchedly poor. They are extremely anxious that their surroundings and home comforts should be improved, yet all the time shirks their work and considers justified in trying to deceive their employer on the ground of the insufficiency of their wages. Such a person does not understand the simplest rudiments of those principles which are the basis of true prosperity, and is not only totally unfit to rise out of their wretchedness, but is actually attracting to themselves a still deeper wretchedness by dwelling in, and acting out, indolent, deceptive, and timorous thoughts.

Here is a rich person who is the victim of a painful and persistent disease as the result of gluttony. They are willing to give large sums of money to get rid of it, but will not sacrifice their gluttonous desires. They want to gratify their taste for rich and unnatural delicacies and have their health as well. Such a person is totally unfit to have health because they have not yet learned the first principles of a healthy life.

Here is an employer of workers who adopts crooked measures to avoid paying the regulation wage, and, in the hope of making larger profits, reduces the wages of their workforce. Such a person is altogether unfit for prosperity, and when they find themselves bankrupt, both as regards reputation and riches, blame circumstances, not knowing that they are the sole author of their condition.

These three cases merely illustrate of the truth

that a person is the causer (though nearly always unconsciously) of their circumstances, and that, whilst aiming at a good end, they are continually frustrating its accomplishment by encouraging thoughts and desires which cannot possibly harmonize with that end. Such cases could be multiplied and varied almost indefinitely, but this is not necessary, so resolve to trace the action of the laws of thought in your own mind and life, and until this is done, mere external facts cannot serve as the grounds of reasoning.

However, circumstances are so complicated, thought is so deeply rooted, and the conditions of happiness vary so, vastly with individuals, that your entire inner-condition (although it may be known to you) cannot be judged by another from the external aspect of your life alone. You may be honest in certain directions, yet suffer privations; you may be dishonest in certain directions, yet acquire wealth; but the conclusion usually formed that you failed *because of your particular honesty,* and that you might, *prospers because of your particular dishonesty,* is the result of a superficial judgment, which assumes that your dishonesty is almost totally corrupt, and that your honesty is almost entirely virtuous. In the light of a deeper knowledge and wider experience, such judgment is found to be erroneous. You may be dishonest but have some admirable virtues, which others do not possess; and you may be honest but have some obnoxious vices. Your honesty reaps the good results of your honest thoughts and acts; but also bring upon you the sufferings, which your vices produce. Your dishonesty likewise garners your own suffering and happiness.

It is pleasing to human vanity to believe that one suffers because of one's virtue; but not until you have eradicated every sickly, bitter, and impure thought from your mind, and washed every corrupt stain from your character, can you be in a position to know and declare that your sufferings are the result of good, and not of bad qualities; and on the way to, yet long before you have reached, that supreme perfection, you will have found, working in your mind and life, the Great Law which is absolutely just, and which cannot, therefore, give good for evil or evil for good. Possessed of such knowledge, you will then know, looking back upon your past ignorance and blindness, that your life is, and always was, justly ordered, and that all your past experiences, good and bad, were the equitable outworking of your evolving, yet unevolved self.

Good thoughts and actions can never produce bad results; bad thoughts and actions can never produce good results. This is but saying that nothing can come from corn but corn, nothing from nettles but nettles. You understand this law in the natural world, and work with it; but do you understand it in the mental and moral world (though its operation there is just as simple and undeviating), and, therefore, you might not co-operate with it.

Suffering is *always* the effect of wrong thought in some direction. It is an indication that you are out of harmony with yourself and with the Law of your being. The sole and supreme use of suffering is to purify, to burn out all that is useless and impure. Suffering ceases for the person who is pure. There could be no purpose in refining gold after the dross had been removed, and a perfectly pure and enlightened being should not suffer.

The circumstances, which you encounter suffering, are the result of your own mental disharmony. The circumstances, which you encounter well-being and contentment, are the result of your own mental harmony. Well-being and contentment, not material possessions, is the measure of right thought; wretchedness, not lack of material possessions, is the measure of wrong thought. You may be cursed and rich or may be blessed and poor. Well-being, contentment and riches are only joined together when the riches are rightly and wisely used, and; the poor only descends into wretchedness when they regard their lot as a burden unjustly imposed.

Indigence and indulgence are the two extremes of wretchedness. They are both equally unnatural and the result of mental chaos. You are not rightly conditioned until you are a happy, healthy, and prosperous being; and happiness, health, and prosperity are the result of a harmonious adjustment of the inner with the outer, of you with your surroundings.

You only begin to be a mature person when you cease to whine and revile, and commence to search for the hidden justice which regulates your life. And, as you adapt your mind to that regulating factor, you cease to accuse others as the cause of your condition, and build yourself up in strong and noble thoughts; cease to kick against circumstances, but begin to *use* them as aids to your more rapid progress, and as a means of discovering the hidden powers and possibilities within yourself.

Law, not confusion, is the dominating principle in the universe; justice, not injustice, is the essence and substance of life; and righteousness, not corruption, is the moulding and moving force in the spiritual government of the world. This being so, you have but to right yourself to find that the universe is right; and during the process of putting yourself right, you will find that as you alter your thoughts towards things and other people, things and other people will alter towards you.

The proof of this truth is in every person, and it, therefore, admits of easy investigation by systematic introspection and self-analysis. When you radically alter your thoughts, you will be astonished at the rapid transformation it will effect in the material conditions of your life. Others imagine that thought can be kept secret, but it cannot; it rapidly crystallizes into habit, and habit solidifies into circumstance. Base thoughts crystallize into habits of drunkenness and sensuality, which solidify into circumstances of destitution and disease: impure thoughts of every kind crystallize into debilitating and confusing habits, which solidify into distracting and adverse circumstances: thoughts of fear, doubt, and indecision crystallize into weak, immature, and irresolute habits, which solidify into circumstances of failure, poverty, and slavish dependence: lazy thoughts crystallize into habits of uncleanliness and dishonesty, which solidify into circumstances of foulness and beggary: hateful and condemnatory thoughts crystallize into habits of accusation and violence, which solidify into circumstances of injury and persecution: selfish thoughts of all kinds crystallize into habits of self-seeking, which solidify into circumstances more or less distressing. On the other hand, beautiful thoughts of all kinds crystallize into habits of grace and kindliness, which solidify into genial and sunny circumstances: pure thoughts crystallize into habits of temperance and self-control, which solidify into circumstances of repose and peace: thoughts of courage, self-reliance, and decision crystallize into valorous habits, which solidify into circumstances of success, plenty, and freedom: energetic thoughts crystallize into habits of cleanliness and industry, which solidify into circumstances of pleasantness: gentle and forgiving thoughts crystallize into habits of gentleness, which solidify into protective and preservative circumstances: loving and unselfish thoughts crystallize into habits of self-forgetfulness for others, which solidify into circumstances of sure and abiding prosperity and true riches.

A particular train of thought persisted in, be it good or bad, cannot fail to produce its results on the character and circumstances. You cannot *directly* choose your circumstances, but you can choose your thoughts, and so indirectly, yet surely, shape your circumstances.

Nature helps you to the gratification of the thoughts, which you most encourage, and opportunities are presented which will most speedily bring to the surface both the good and evil thoughts.

When you cease your corrupt thoughts, all the world will soften towards you, and be ready to help; when you put away your weak and sickly thoughts, and lo, opportunities will spring up on every hand to aid your strong resolve; when you encourage good thoughts, and no hard fate shall bind you down to wretchedness and shame. The world is your kaleidoscope, and the varying combinations of colours, which at every succeeding moment it presents to you the exquisitely adjusted pictures of your ever-moving thoughts.

"So you will be what you Will to be;
Let failure find its false content
In that poor word, 'environment,'
But spirit scorns it, and is free.

"It masters time, it conquers space;
It cowes that boastful trickster, Chance,
And bids the tyrant Circumstance
Uncrown, and fill a worker's place.

"Your inner Will, that force unseen,
The offspring of a deathless Soul,
Can hew a way to any goal,
Though walls of granite intervene.

"You'll be not impatient in delays
But wait as one who understands;
When spirit rises and commands
The gods are ready to obey."

EFFECT OF THOUGHT ON HEALTH AND THE BODY

THE body is the servant of your mind. It obeys the operations of your mind, whether deliberately chosen or automatically expressed. At the bidding of unlawful thoughts, the body sinks rapidly into disease and decay; at the command of glad and beautiful thoughts, it becomes clothed with youthfulness and beauty.

Disease and health, like circumstances, are rooted in your thoughts. Sickly thoughts will express themselves through a sickly body. Thoughts of fear have been known to kill as speedily as a bullet, and they are continually killing thousands of people just as surely though less rapidly. If you live in fear of disease you are going to be affected. Anxiety quickly demoralizes your whole body, and lays it open to the entrance of disease; while impure thoughts, even if not physically indulged, will soon shatter your nervous system.

Strong, pure, and happy thoughts build up your body in vigour and grace. The body is a delicate and mouldable instrument, which responds readily to your thoughts by which it is impressed, and habits of thought will produce their own effects, good or bad, upon it.

You will continue to have impure and poisoned

blood, so long as you propagate unclean thoughts. Out of a clean heart comes a clean life and a clean body. Out of a defiled mind proceeds a defiled life and a corrupt body. Thought is the fount of action, life, and manifestation; make the fountain pure, and all will be pure.

Change of diet will not help you if you will not change your thoughts. When you make your thoughts pure, you no longer desire impure food.

Clean thoughts make clean habits. The so-called saint who does not wash their body is not a saint. If you strengthened and purified your thoughts you do not need to consider the malevolent microbe.

If you would protect your body, guard your mind. If you would renew your body, beautify your mind. Thoughts of malice, envy, disappointment, despondency, rob your body of its health and grace. A sour face does not come by chance; it is made by sour thoughts. Wrinkles that mar are drawn by folly, obsession, and pride.

For example, consider a person of ninety-six who has the bright, innocent face of a youth. Or, another well under middle age whose face is drawn into inharmonious contours. The one is the result of a pleasant and sunny disposition; the other is the outcome of fervour and discontent.

As you cannot have a sweet and wholesome abode unless you admit the air and sunshine freely into your rooms, so a strong body and a bright, happy, or serene countenance can only result from the free admittance into your mind of thoughts of joy and goodwill and serenity.

On the faces of the aged there are wrinkles made by sympathy, others by strong and pure thought, and others are carved by obsession: who cannot distinguish them? With those who have lived righteously, age is calm, peaceful, and softly mellowed, like the setting sun. Or, like a philosopher who on their deathbed is not old except in years. Dying as sweetly and peacefully as they had lived.

You can have no better physician than cheerful thoughts for dissipating the ills of your body; there is no comforter to compare with goodwill for dispersing the shadows of grief and sorrow. For you to live continually in thoughts of ill will, cynicism, suspicion, and envy, is to be confined in a self-made prison. But to think well of all, to be cheerful with all, to patiently learn to find the good in all—such unselfish thoughts are the very portals of heaven, and to dwell day by day in thoughts of peace toward every creature will bring abounding peace into your possession.

THOUGHT AND PURPOSE

UNTIL thought is linked with purpose there is no intelligent accomplishment. With the majority, the sudden powerful thought is allowed to "drift" upon the ocean of life. Aimlessness is a vice and such drifting must not continue if you desire to steer clear of catastrophe and destruction.

If you have no central purpose in your life you fall easy prey to petty worries, fears, troubles, and self-pity, all of which are indications of weakness, which lead, just as surely as deliberately planned misdemeanours (though by a different route), to failure, unhappiness, and loss, for weakness cannot persist in a power evolving universe.

You should conceive of a legitimate purpose in your heart, and set out to accomplish it. You should make this purpose the centralizing point of your thoughts. It may take the form of a noble ideal, or it may be a worldly object, according to your nature at the time; but whichever it is, you should steadily focus your thought-forces upon the object, which you have set before yourself. You should make this purpose your supreme duty and should devote yourself to its attainment, not allowing your thoughts to wander away into short-lived fancies, longings, and imaginings. This is the royal road to self-control and true concentration of thought. Even if you fail again and again to accomplish your purpose (as you necessarily must until weakness is overcome), the *strength of character gained* will be the measure of *your true* success, and this will form a new starting-point for future power and triumph.

If you are not prepared for the establishment of a *great* purpose you should fix your thoughts upon the faultless performance of your duty, no matter how insignificant that task may appear. Only in this way can your thoughts be gathered and focussed, and resolution and energy be developed, which being done, there is nothing which may not be accomplished.

As the weakest soul, knows its own weakness, and believing this truth *that strength can only be developed by effort and practice,* you will, thus believing, at once begin to exert yourself, and, adding effort to effort, patience to patience, and strength to strength, will never cease to develop, and will, at last, grow divinely strong.

As the physically weak person can make themselves strong by careful and patient training, so you, of weak thoughts can make yourself strong by exercising yourself in the art of right thinking.

Put away aimlessness and weakness, and begin to think with purpose, this is to enter the ranks of those strong ones who only recognize failure as one of the pathways to attainment; who make all conditions serve them, and who think strongly, attempt fearlessly, and accomplish masterfully.

Having conceived of your purpose, you should mentally mark out a *straight* pathway to its achievement, looking neither to the right nor the left. Doubts and fears should be rigorously excluded; they are disintegrating elements, which break up the straight line of effort, rendering it crooked, ineffectual, useless. Thoughts of doubt and fear never accomplished anything, and never can. They always lead to failure. Purpose, energy, the power to do, and all strong thoughts cease when doubt and fear creep in.

The will to do springs from the knowledge that you *can* do. Doubt and fear are the great enemies of knowledge, and when you encourage them, those that you do not slay defeat you at every step.

When you have conquered doubt and fear you have conquered failure. Your every thought is allied with power, and all difficulties are bravely met and wisely overcome. Your purposes are seasonably planted, and they bloom and bring forth fruit, which does not fall prematurely to the ground.

Thought allied fearlessly to purpose becomes a creative force: You *know* this is ready to become something higher and stronger than a mere bundle of wavering thoughts and fluctuating sensations; when you *do* this you have become the conscious and intelligent wielder of your mental powers.

THE THOUGHT-FACTOR IN ACHIEVEMENT

ALL that you achieve and all that you fail to achieve is the direct result of your own thoughts. In a justly ordered universe, where the loss of equilibrium would mean total destruction, individual responsibility must be absolute. Your weakness and strength, purity and impurity, are your own, and not another person's; they are brought about by yourself, and not by another; and they can only be altered by you, never by another. Your condition is also your own, and not another person's. Your suffering and happiness are evolved from within. As you think, so you are; as you continue to think, so you remain.

A strong person cannot help a weaker person unless the weaker is willing to be helped, and even then the weaker person must become strong of themselves; they must, by their own efforts, develop the strength which they admire in another. In truth, no-one but you can alter your condition.

It has been usual for people to think and to say, "Many are exploited because one is an oppressor; let us hate the oppressor." Now, however, there is amongst an increasing few a tendency to reverse this judgment, and to say, "One is an oppressor because many are exploited; let us despise the exploited."

The truth is that oppressor and exploited are co-operators in ignorance, and, while seeming to afflict each other, are in reality afflicting themselves. A perfect Knowledge perceives the action of law in the weakness of the oppressed and the misapplied power of the oppressor; a perfect Love, seeing the suffering, which both states entail, condemns neither; a perfect Compassion embraces both oppressor and oppressed.

Those who have conquered weakness, and have put away all selfish thoughts, belongs neither to oppressor nor oppressed. They are free.

You can only rise, conquer, and achieve by lifting up your thoughts. You can only remain weak, and abject, and miserable by refusing to lift up your thoughts.

Before you can achieve anything, even in worldly things, You must lift your thoughts above mindless animal indulgence. You may not, in order to succeed, give up all animality and selfishness, by any means; but a portion of it must, at least, be sacrificed. If your first thought is degrading indulgence and could neither think clearly nor plan methodically; you could not find and develop your latent resources, and would fail in any undertaking. Not having commenced to willfully control your thoughts, you are not in a position to control your obligations and to adopt serious responsibilities. You are not fit to act independently and stand alone. But, you are limited only by the thoughts which you choose.

There can be no progress, no achievement without sacrifice, and your worldly success will be in the measure that you sacrifice your confused unrefined thoughts and fix your mind on the development of your plans, and the strengthening of your resolution and self-reliance. And the higher you lift your thoughts, the more fearless, upright, and virtuous you become, the greater will be your success, the more worthy and enduring will be your achievements.

The universe does not favour the greedy, the dishonest, the vicious, although on the mere surface it may sometimes appear to do so; it helps the honest, the magnanimous, the virtuous. All the great Teachers of the ages have declared this in varying forms, and to prove and know it you have but to persist in making yourself more and more virtuous by lifting up your thoughts.

Intellectual achievements are the result of thought dedicated to the search for knowledge, or for all that is beautiful and true in life and nature. Such achievements may be sometimes connected with vanity and ambition, but they are not the outcome of those characteristics; they are the natural outgrowth of long and arduous effort, and of pure and unselfish thoughts.

Spiritual achievements are the fulfilment of righteous aspirations. When you live constantly in the creation of noble and lofty thoughts and dwell upon all that is pure and unselfish, you will, as surely as the sun reaches its zenith and the moon its full, become wise and noble in character and rise into a position of influence, well-being and contentment.

Achievement, of whatever kind, is the crown of effort, the diadem of thought. By the aid of self-control, resolution, purity, righteousness, and well-directed thought you ascend; by the aid of brutishness, indolence, impurity, corruption, and confusion of thought you descend.

You may rise to high success in the world, and even to lofty altitudes in the divine realm, and again descend into weakness and wretchedness by allowing arrogant, selfish, and corrupt thoughts to take possession of you.

Victories attained by right thought can only be maintained by watchfulness. If you give way when success is assured you will rapidly fall back into failure.

All achievements, whether in the business, intellectual, or spiritual world, are the result of definitely directed thought, they are governed by the same law and are of the same method; the only difference lies in the object of attainment.

You, who would accomplish little, must sacrifice little; You, who would achieve much, must sacrifice much; You, who would attain highly must sacrifice greatly.

VISIONS AND IDEALS

THE dreamers are the saviours of the world. As the visible world is sustained by the invisible, so people, through all their trials, sins and sordid inclinations, are nourished by the beautiful visions of those solitary dreamers. Humanity cannot forget its dreamers; it cannot let their ideals fade and die; it lives in them; it knows them as the *realities* which it will one day see and know.

Composer, sculptor, painter, poet, prophet, sage, these are the makers of the world they leave, the architects of heaven. The world is beautiful because they have lived; without them, labouring humanity would perish.

When you cherish a beautiful vision, a lofty ideal in your heart, you will one day realize it. Columbus cherished a vision of another world, and he discovered it; Copernicus fostered the vision of many worlds and a wider universe, and he revealed it; Buddha beheld the vision of a spiritual world of stainless beauty and perfect peace, and he entered into it.

Cherish your visions; cherish your ideals; cherish the music that stirs in your heart, the beauty that forms in your mind, the loveliness that drapes your purest thoughts, for out of them will grow all delightful conditions, all, heavenly environment; of these, if you but remain true to them, your world will, at last, be built.

To desire is to obtain; to aspire is to achieve. Shall your basest desires receive the fullest measure of gratification, and your purest aspirations starve for lack of sustenance? Such is not the Law: such a condition of things can never occur: "ask and receive."

Dream lofty dreams, and as you dream, so shall you become. Your Vision is the promise of what you shall one day be; your Ideal is the prophecy of what you shall at last unveil.

The greatest achievement was at first and for a time a dream. The oak sleeps in the acorn; the bird waits in the egg; and in the highest vision of the soul, a waking angel stirs, at last, here are the seedlings of realities.

Your circumstances may be uncongenial, but they shall not long remain so if you but perceive an Ideal and strive to reach it. You cannot travel *within* and stand still *without.*

Here is a youth hard pressed by poverty and hard work; confined long hours in an unhealthy workshop; unschooled, and lacking all the arts of refinement. But dreams of better things; thinks of intelligence, of refinement, of grace and beauty. Conceives of, mentally builds up, an ideal condition of life; the vision of a wider liberty and a larger scope takes possession of the youth; unrest urges the youth to action, and utilizing all their spare time and means, small though they are, to the development of latent powers and resources. Very soon, so altered is their mind that the workshop can no longer hold them. It has become so out of harmony with their mentality that it falls out of their life, like an unwanted garment, it is cast aside, and, with the growth of opportunities, which fit the scope of expanding powers, the youth passes out of it forever. Years later we see this youth as a full-grown adult. We find a master of certain forces of the mind, which wields worldwide influence and almost unequalled power. In their hands they hold the cords of gigantic responsibilities; they speak and lives are changed; people hang upon their words and remould their characters, and, sun-like, becomes the fixed and luminous centre around which innumerable destinies revolve. They have realized the Vision of their youth and have become as one with their Ideal.

As you, too, will realize the Vision (not the idle wish) of your heart, be it base or beautiful, or a mixture of both, for you will always gravitate toward that which you, secretly, most love. Into your hands will be placed the exact results of your own thoughts; you will receive that which you earn; no more, no less. Whatever your present environment may be, you will fall, remain, or rise with your thoughts, your Vision, your Ideal. You will become as small as your controlling desire; as great as your dominant aspiration: in the beautiful words of Stanton Kirkham Davis, "You may be keeping accounts, and presently you shall walk out of the door that for so long has seemed to you the barrier of your ideals, and shall find yourself before an audience—the pen still behind your ear, the ink stains on your fingers and then and there shall pour out the torrent of your inspiration. You may be driving sheep, and you shall wander to the city, a shepherd of the pastures and gazing open-mouthed; shall wander under the intrepid guidance of the spirit into the studio of the master, and after a time they will say, 'I have nothing more to teach you.' And now you have become the master, who did so recently dream of great things while driving sheep. you shall lay down the saw and the plane to take upon yourself the regeneration of the world."

The thoughtless, the ignorant, and the indolent, seeing only the apparent effects of things and not the things themselves, talk of luck, of fortune, and chance. Seeing you grow rich, they might say, "How lucky you are!" Observing you becoming intellectual, they exclaim, "How highly favoured you are!" And noting your virtuous character and wide influence, they remark, "How chance aids you at every turn!" They do not see the trials and failures and struggles which you have voluntarily encountered in order to gain your experience; have no knowledge of the sacrifices you have made, of the undaunted efforts you have put forth, of the faith you have exercised, that you might overcome the apparently insurmountable, and realize the Vision of your heart. They do not know the darkness and the heartaches; they only see the light and joy, and call it "luck". They do not see the long and arduous journey, but only behold the pleasant goal, and call it "good fortune," they do not understand the process, but only perceive the result, and call it chance.

In all your affairs there are *efforts,* and there are *results,* and the strength of the effort is the measure of the result. Chance it is not. Gifts, powers, material, intellectual, and spiritual possessions are the fruits of effort; they are thoughts completed, objects accomplished, visions realized.

The Vision that you glorify in your mind, the Ideal that you enthrone in your heart—this you will build your life by, this you will become.

SERENITY

CALMNESS of mind is one of the beautiful jewels of wisdom. It is the result of long and patient effort in self-control. Its presence is an indication of ripened experience, and of a more than ordinary knowledge of the laws and operations of thought.

You become calm in the measure that you understand yourself as a thought evolved being, for such knowledge necessitates the understanding of others as the result of thought, and as you develop a right understanding and see more and more clearly the internal association of things by the action of cause and effect you cease to fuss and fume and worry and grieve, and remain poised, steadfast, serene.

As a calm person, you have learned how to govern yourself, know how to adapt yourself to others; and they, in turn, respect your inner strength, and feel that they can learn from you and rely upon you. The more tranquil you become, the greater is your success, your influence, your power for good. Even as an ordinary trader you will find your business prosperity increases as you develop a greater self-control and composure, for people will always prefer to deal with a person whose demeanour is very composed.

The strong, calm person is always loved and revered. You are like a shade-giving tree in a thirsty land or a sheltering rock in a storm. "Who does not love a tranquil heart, a sweet-tempered, balanced life? It does not matter whether it rains or shines, or what changes come whilst you are possessing these blessings, for you are always beloved, serene, and calm. That exquisite poise of character, which you enjoy, serenity is the last lesson of culture, the fruitage of the soul. Serenity is as precious as wisdom, more to be desired than gold—yes, than even fine gold. How insignificant mere money-seeking looks in comparison with a serene life—a life that dwells in the ocean of Truth, beneath the waves, beyond the reach of tempests, in the Eternal Calm!

How many people you know who sour their lives, who ruin all that is sweet and beautiful by explosive tempers, who destroy their poise of character, and make bad blood! It is a question, do the great majority of people ruin their lives and mar their happiness by lack of self-control? Those you desire to meet in life are those who are well balanced, who have that exquisite poise which is characteristic of the finished character!

Yes, humanity surges with uncontrolled passion, is tumultuous with ungoverned grief, is blown about by anxiety and doubt. You wish to become like the wise person, only then will your thoughts be controlled and purified, make the winds and the storms of your soul obey you.

As a tempest-tossed soul, wherever you might be, under whatsoever conditions you may live, you know this, in the ocean of life the isles of Well-being and Contentment are smiling, and the sunny shore of your ideal awaits your coming. You must keep your hand firmly upon the helm of thought. In the growling of your soul lies the commanding Master; you do but sleep: awake. Self-control is strength; Right Thought is mastery; Calmness is power. Say to your heart, "Peace, be still!"